What did knights wear in the day?

Disney BOOKS BY MAIL

DK Direct Limited
Managing Art Editor Eljay Crompton
Senior Editor Rosemary McCormick
Writer Rachel Wright
Illustrators The Alvin White Studios and Richard Manning
Designers Wayne Blades, Veneta Bullen, Richard Clemson,
Sarah Goodwin, Diane Klein, Sonia Whillock

Contents

Who were the first artists?

They were cave dwellers who lived thousands and thousands of years ago. They scratched and painted pictures on cave walls and ceilings, and made small models out of animal bone. Unlike us, they had to make their own paints because store-bought paints hadn't been invented!

Cave rave
What kind of music did cave men like best?
Rock 'n' Roll.

Hand carving
The earliest artists carved images of the wild animals they hunted for food.

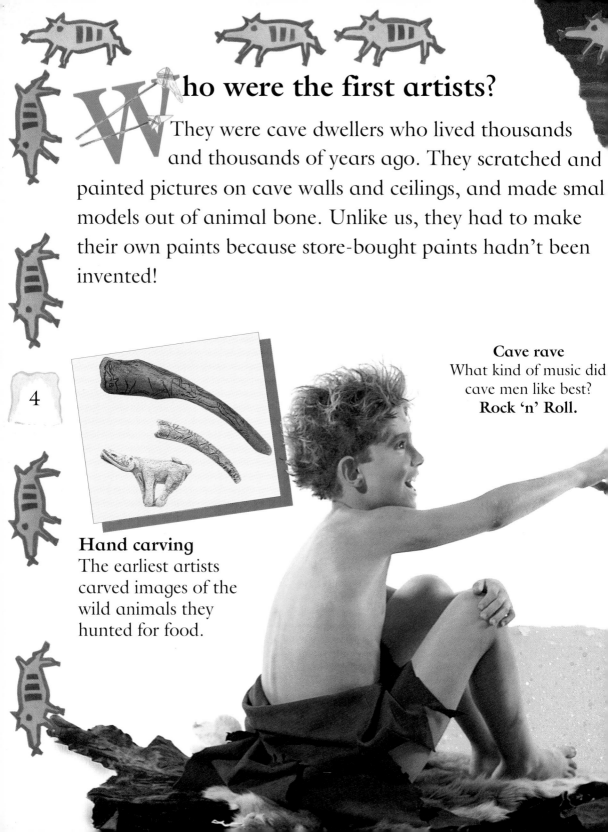

Cave art facts

☞ Cave artists used paints made from animals and plants. They made paintbrushes from twigs and animal hairs.

☞ Early artists lit their dark caves by burning animal fat in stone lamps.

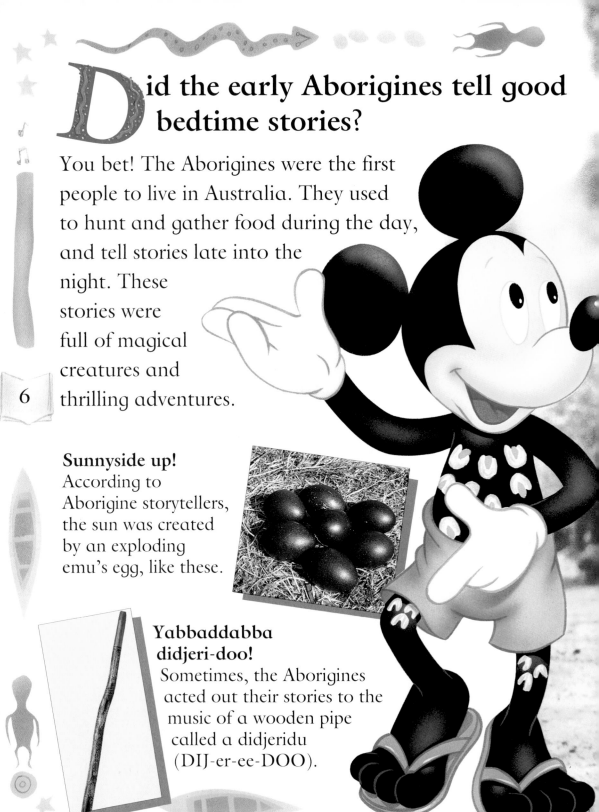

Did the early Aborigines tell good bedtime stories?

You bet! The Aborigines were the first people to live in Australia. They used to hunt and gather food during the day, and tell stories late into the night. These stories were full of magical creatures and thrilling adventures.

6

Sunnyside up!
According to Aborigine storytellers, the sun was created by an exploding emu's egg, like these.

Yabbaddabba didjeri-doo!
Sometimes, the Aborigines acted out their stories to the music of a wooden pipe called a didjeridu (DIJ-er-ee-DOO).

Changing continents

☞ Australia has not always been an island. About 200 million years ago it was joined to India, Antarctica, Africa, and South America.

☞ Before going out on a hunt, Aborigines used to do a dance which imitated the animal they were going to hunt.

Did the ancient Egyptians dress for dinner?

They sure did! In fact both men and women often spent all afternoon just getting ready to have dinner with friends. First, they rubbed oils into their skins and shaved their bodies. Then, they put on their make-up, jewelry, and wigs. Finally, they put cones of scented grease on top of their heads. As the evening wore on, the grease melted and soaked everyone's clothes in sweet-smelling oil.

What a drag!
The ancient Egyptians buried their kings in huge stone pyramids. These pyramids took years and years to make because the builders had to drag each block of stone – which weighed as much as 100 people – into place by hand.

8

Eat up!

Rich Egyptians ate
many different foods.
Poor Egyptians
mostly ate bread,
vegetables,
and fish.

Sand sandwiches

Egyptian bread was very
gritty because sand often
blew into the flour as it
was being ground. Eating
sandy bread each day
wore down everyone's
teeth and gave them
terrible toothaches!

Did the Greeks go to the movies long ago?

No, because movies hadn't been invented in ancient Greece. But they did go to the theater. Greek plays were usually part of religious festivals. They were very, very popular. People would take a packed lunch and spend the whole day watching one play after another.

Seeing is believing

Ancient Greek theaters were very large. To help those at the back see what was going on, the actors wore huge masks with large, open mouths.

Building experts

The ancient Greeks lived over 2,000 years ago. They were good builders. Parts of their buildings are still standing in Greece today.

Excuse me!
What do you do
if an elephant
sits in front of you
at the theater?
Miss the play!

Ancient athletic facts

☞ Did you know that the ancient Greeks invented the Olympic games? Every four years, lots of them stopped work and hurried off to a place called Olympia. There they watched all sorts of exciting events, including bareback riding and chariot races.

Did the Vikings go on vacation?

No, but they did travel to raid and trade. The Vikings were pirates, daring explorers, and smart traders all rolled into one. They lived in Scandinavia more than 1,000 years ago. They were always on the lookout for unguarded towns to raid. No wonder most people ran for cover whenever the Vikings were heading their way!

Dressing up
Viking warriors wore special helmets like this when they went to battle.

Viking facts

☞ The Vikings were expert boat builders. Their boats often had scary-looking carvings of dragons' heads on the front.

☞ When the Vikings went to sea, the sailors slept on the decks. They kept warm in large sleeping bags made of leather.

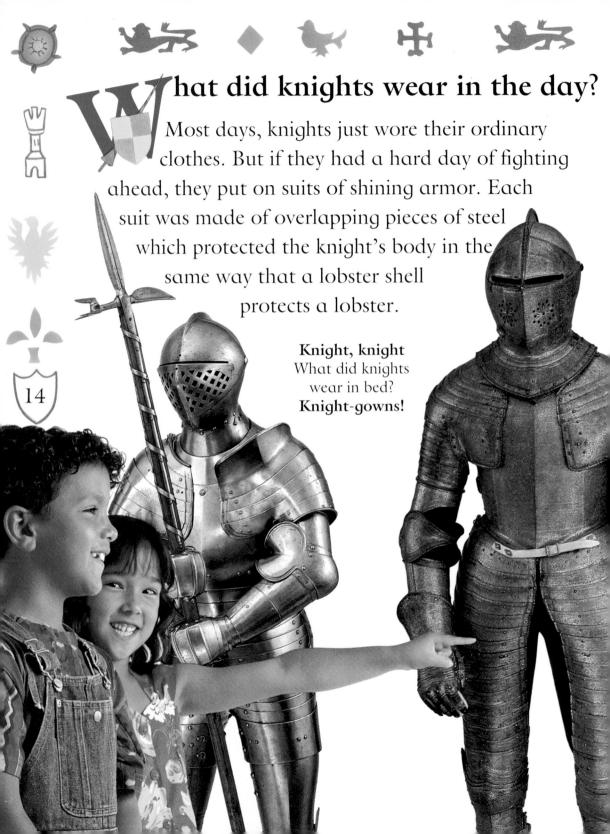

What did knights wear in the day?

Most days, knights just wore their ordinary clothes. But if they had a hard day of fighting ahead, they put on suits of shining armor. Each suit was made of overlapping pieces of steel which protected the knight's body in the same way that a lobster shell protects a lobster.

Knight, knight
What did knights wear in bed?
Knight-gowns!

14

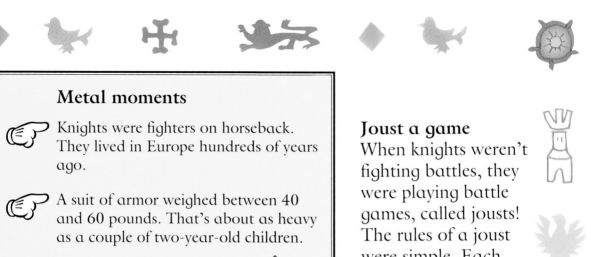

Metal moments

👉 Knights were fighters on horseback. They lived in Europe hundreds of years ago.

👉 A suit of armor weighed between 40 and 60 pounds. That's about as heavy as a couple of two-year-old children.

Joust a game

When knights weren't fighting battles, they were playing battle games, called jousts! The rules of a joust were simple. Each knight had to charge toward the other and try to hit him with a wooden pole!

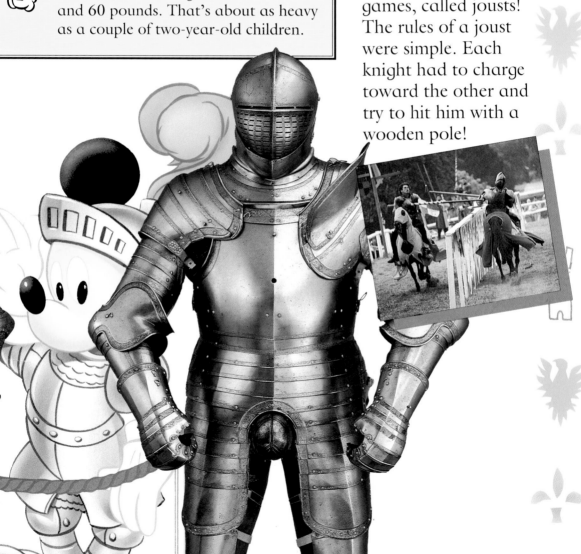

Did castles have bathrooms?

Unfortunately, no! When someone wanted a bath, water had to be collected from a well. It was heated over a fire and poured into a wooden tub. Filling a bath like this took a long time. So, when the first person got out, others used the tub in turns. The last one out of the tub must have been even dirtier than when he got in!

Home sweet home
Castles were forts as well as homes. They were built long ago to protect wealthy families and their servants and knights.

Haunted house

Some say Windsor castle, in England, is haunted by the ghost of an English King named Charles I.

Castle facts

☞ Castles didn't have flushing toilets. Instead they had chutes which ran down inside the castle wall and out into a pit. Daring soldiers sometimes managed to sneak into enemy castles by climbing up these chutes.

Did early native Americans talk long distance?

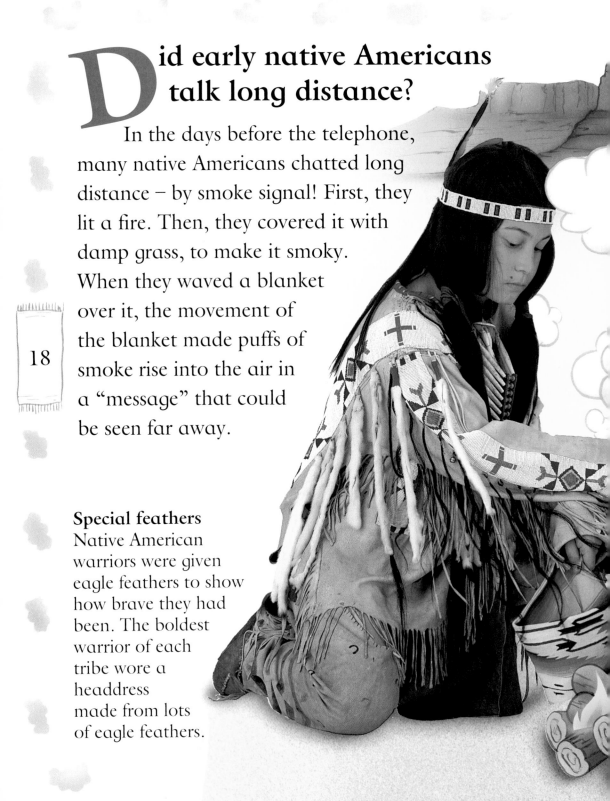

In the days before the telephone, many native Americans chatted long distance – by smoke signal! First, they lit a fire. Then, they covered it with damp grass, to make it smoky. When they waved a blanket over it, the movement of the blanket made puffs of smoke rise into the air in a "message" that could be seen far away.

18

Special feathers
Native American warriors were given eagle feathers to show how brave they had been. The boldest warrior of each tribe wore a headdress made from lots of eagle feathers.

Hand signs

Early native Americans
lived in groups called tribes.
Each tribe spoke its own
language. But they also
used hand signs.

Survival facts

Many early Americans
survived by hunting the
buffalo. They used its
meat for food and its skin
for making clothes.

Did the Aztecs go to school?

Yes, but their classes weren't anything like today's. The Aztecs ruled the largest empire ever seen in Central America. Most boys were taught how to fight so they could protect the empire. Only those boys and girls who were to be priests were taught "school" subjects such as math.

Brave fighters
The bravest Aztec warriors of all were called Eagle and Jaguar knights. They wore animal skins and feathers and carried wooden clubs.

Picture this
Priests and noblemen wrote by drawing pictures.

Amazing Aztec facts

☞ The Aztecs loved drinking cold chocolate. In fact, one Aztec emperor had 50 jars of the drink made every day – just for himself!

☞ The Aztec empire came to an end nearly 500 years ago, when it was conquered by Spain.

How did the pilgrims do their laundry?

By hand! Probably one of the first things the pilgrims did when they reached America in 1620, was to start washing. Their sea voyage from England had taken about two and a half months, so they had plenty of laundry to get through!

The first Thanksgiving
Once they had begun to settle in America, the pilgrims held a big thanksgiving feast. They invited local native Americans to join them in this celebration.

Welcome home

☞ The pilgrims were some of the first English-speaking people to settle in America. They were helped in their new life by a native American called Squanto. He showed them how to plant corn and build canoes.

How did Buffalo Bill write to his mom?

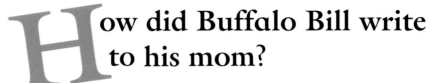

Buffalo Bill worked for a mail company called the Pony Express, so he probably delivered his letters himself. In the days before railroads and mail trucks, the Pony Express used teams of riders to gallop across America. The service worked like a relay race. Each rider rode for about 75 miles, then threw his mailbags to a new rider, who took his place.

Telegraph take-over
The Pony Express only lasted 18 months. It ended in 1861 when the telegraph system was built.

Horse humor
What did the pony say
when he coughed?
**Excuse me, I'm just
a little hoarse!**

Mr. Bill
Buffalo Bill was a great buffalo
hunter and showman. He was
called "Buffalo" because he
supplied workers with buffalo
meat while they built America's
first railroads.

25

Get a move on facts!

☞ Pony Express riders took
about eight to ten days to
carry mail from Missouri to
California. That doesn't
seem very speedy, does it?
Yet it was a lot faster than
any other mail service at
that time.

Have people always used money?

Not always. Long, long ago, everyone shopped by swapping something they had for something they wanted. Over time, this changed, and many people agreed to take valuable things, such as cattle and cloth, as "money." Paying for groceries with a herd of cattle wasn't always easy though. So coins and paper money were invented, instead.

Odd change
Thousands of years ago, people in China used coins shaped like knives.

Chop and change

When Europeans first settled in North America, they used coins from Spain. To make change, they chopped the coins into pie-shaped pieces, called bits.

MICKEY'S Mind teaser

Long ago, people wore special headdresses.
Can you remember who wore what?

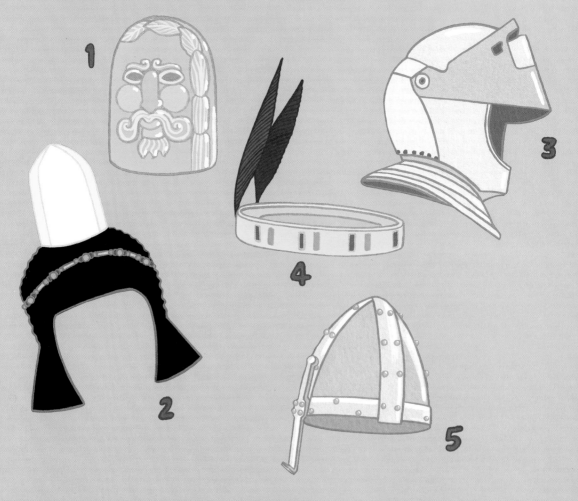

For Mary Briggs
M.W.

For Edwina
P.B.

Text copyright © 1986 Martin Waddell
Illustrations copyright © 1986 Patrick Benson
First published in the United States of America
in 1987 by Philomel Books, a member of The Putnam
Publishing Group, 51 Madison Avenue, New York, NY 10010.
First published in 1986 by Walker Books Ltd, London.
Printed and bound in Italy. All Rights reserved.
ISBN 0-399-21380-5
First Impression

Library of Congress Cataloging-in-Publication Data
Waddell, Martin.   The tough princess.
Summary: A spunky princess with a mind of her
own resists her parents' plans to ensnare
a prince for her and rides forth to
adventures of her choosing.
[1. Fairy tales] I. Benson, Patrick, ill.
II. Title. PZ8.W115To   1986   [E]   86-8178

THE TOUGH PRINCESS

written by

Martin Waddell

illustrated by

Patrick Benson

PHILOMEL BOOKS

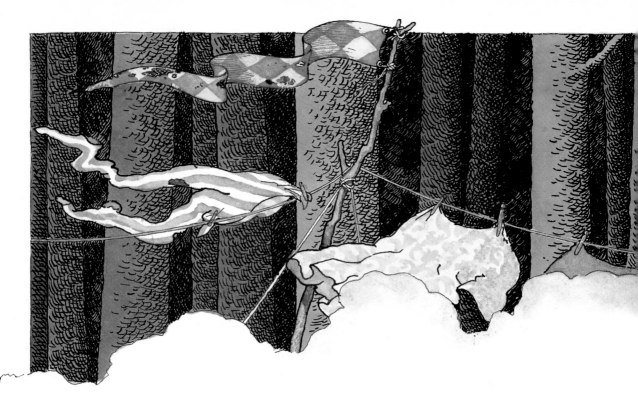

Once upon a time there lived a King and
a Queen who weren't very good at it.
They kept losing wars and kingdoms,
and ended up living in a caravan
parked beside a deep dark wood.
The King is the one with the frying pan.
The Queen is the one with the hammer,
trying to fix the roof.

One day the Queen told the King
that she was going to have a baby.
'Have a boy!' commanded the King.
'He will grow up to be a hero,
marry a rich princess and
restore all of our fortunes!'
'Good idea!' said the Queen.
But when the baby came…

…it was a girl!

'Never mind,' said the King.

'She will grow up to be
a beautiful princess.
I will annoy a bad fairy and
get the Princess into trouble. Then
a handsome prince will rescue her, and
we'll all go off and live in his castle!'

'Good thinking!' said the Queen.

'We'll call her Rosamund.'

'Ba!' said Rosamund.

The Princess grew up and up and up and up,
until at last there wasn't room
in the caravan to hold her.
The King got her a tent and
pitched it outside.
'It's time you were married, Rosamund,'
the King told the Princess
on her seventeenth birthday.
'Yes, Dad,' said the Princess, 'but…'
'I'll go off and arrange it,' said the King.

The King went off into the deep dark wood
to annoy some bad fairies.
The first fairy the King met was a good one.
She didn't even get angry
when the King
called her names.

The second fairy was bad, but
she was only a beginner.
She turned the King into a frog
for making faces at her cat,
but the spell wore off.

The third fairy was **very** bad.

Here she is.

The King was very rude to her.

'Aha!' cried the Bad Fairy.

'What do you love most in the world?'

'My daughter Rosamund!'
cried the King hopefully.
'Then I will cast a spell on
her!' cackled the Bad Fairy,
who wasn't very bright, and
she darted off to do it.
'Good-eee!' cried the King, because
his get-the-princess-a-rich-prince
plan was working.

The Bad Fairy came upon Princess Rosamund
picking buttercups in a glade.
'Aha!' she cried. 'I am the Bad Fairy,
come to cast a spell on you.

Seven years shall you lie
Till a prince comes riding by…'

Bop! went Princess Rosamund, and
she knocked the Bad Fairy out,
bent her false teeth and
busted her glasses.

'You rotten, ungrateful thing, Rosamund!'
said the Queen, picking up the Bad Fairy.
'I'll find my prince my own way!'
said Princess Rosamund.
The next day she borrowed the King's bike
and rode off to seek her prince.

Rosamund had a lot of adventures.
She slew dragons and great serpents and
black knights. She rescued several princes
who were quite rich, but she didn't like them,
and so she threw them back.
She did all the things a heroine ought to do,
but she didn't find her prince.

Finally, Princess Rosamund grew tired
of rescuing princes and killing dragons,
and her front wheel buckled in a fight
with a hundred-headed thing.
So she set off
sadly for home,
carrying her bicycle.

'Hello, Mom. Hello, Dad. Hello, Bad Fairy,'
said Princess Rosamund when she got home.
'Where's your prince then?' said the King and
the Queen and the Bad Fairy,
who had moved in by this time.
'Haven't got one,' said Princess Rosamund.
'I'm not going to marry a ninny!'
'What about us!' cried the King and
the Queen and the Bad Fairy.
'What are we supposed to live on if you can't
come up with a prince?'
'That's your problem!' said Princess Rosamund.
'I'm not going to…'
and then she saw the sign.

THIS WAY TO THE
ENCHANTED
PRINCE

'I'm doing this for me!' said Rosamund firmly,
and she set off into the deep dark wood.
'You can look after yourselves!'
She bashed up several goblins and ghouls and
the odd fairy (including several good ones
by mistake), and finally she won her way
through to the Enchanted Castle.
There, on a flower-strewn bed in the castle
lay a beautiful prince.
Rosamund gave him a big kiss.

The beautiful prince opened his eyes, jumped
to his feet, and put up his fists.

Rosamund did too. But before their fists met,
their eyes did.

'What a prince!' she said.

'What a princess!' he said.

It was love at first look. So they biked off
together on the buckled bike and lived happily
ever after. The King and the Queen
lived happily ever after too,
and the Bad Fairy
got even worse.